I0490669

MASTERING THE EFFECTIVE AND SUCCESSFUL LEADER MINDSET

John Sanchez

Copyright © 2023 John Sanchez

All rights reserved

The characters and events portrayed in this book are fictitious. Any similarity to real persons, living or dead, is coincidental and not intended by the author.

No part of this book may be reproduced, or stored in a retrieval system, or transmitted in any form or by any means, electronic, mechanical, photocopying, recording, or otherwise, without express written permission of the publisher.

ISBN-13: 9798392001101

Cover design by: Art Painter
Library of Congress Control Number: 2018675309
Printed in the United States of America

To my dearest Dad,

Although you're no longer with me, your legacy lives on in everything I do. Your unwavering support and belief in me gave me the strength and determination to pursue my dreams. Thank you for instilling in me a strong work ethic, the value of integrity, and the importance of always striving for personal growth. This book is a testament to your belief in me, and I hope it makes you proud.

This book is dedicated to you for your unwavering support, encouragement, and inspiration throughout my life.

With all my love and gratitude,

John Sanchez

"A true leader has the confidence to stand alone, the courage to make tough decisions, and the compassion to listen to the needs of others. He does not set out to be a leader but becomes one by the equality of his actions and the integrity of his intent."

DOUGLAS MACARTHUR

CONTENTS

PREFACE: DISCOVERING THE LEADER WITHIN

In writing this book, I draw on my years of experience as a CEO, coach, and mentor to help you develop the mindset and skills you need to become a successful and effective leader. I firmly believe that leadership is not a one-size-fits-all approach and that each individual has their unique style of leading. With that in mind, this book provides various tools, strategies, and insights to apply to your leadership journey. Whether you're an experienced leader looking to enhance your skills or a new manager seeking guidance, this book will help you unlock your full potential as a leader.

Throughout my career, I've been committed to helping people find their purpose and align their actions with their goals to create meaningful change. As a leader, coach, and mentor with over 25 years of experience working with individuals and organizations across various industries, I've seen firsthand the immense impact that effective and successful leadership can have on teams, organizations, and the world. This book, "Mastering the Effective and Successful Leader Mindset," is the culmination of the insights and lessons I've learned along the way.

Becoming a truly effective and successful leader is lifelong, requiring continuous learning, self-reflection, and growth. In this book, I've distilled the core principles and strategies essential for anyone looking to develop their leadership skills, regardless of their industry or background. From exploring the importance of self-awareness and emotional intelligence to navigating the challenges of leading through change and transformation, this comprehensive guide will provide the tools and knowledge you need to become the best leader you can be.

As you embark on your leadership development journey, remember that your unique background, experiences, and perspectives are assets that can help you forge your leadership style. The insights and lessons shared in this book will help you hone your leadership abilities and inspire you to embrace the journey of self-discovery and growth.

You should dive into the book with an open mind, a willingness to learn, and a commitment to self-improvement. In doing so, you'll enhance your leadership abilities and empower and inspire those around you to reach their full potential. I look forward to sharing this journey with you and witnessing the incredible impact you can have as an effective and successful leader.

Wishing you success and fulfillment on your leadership journey,

John Sanchez
April 2023

CHAPTER 1.
INTRODUCTION

Welcome to "Mastering the Effective and Successful Leader Mindset." In this comprehensive guide, we will explore leadership's vital role in today's world, define effective and successful leadership, and begin your journey to mastering leadership skills. Ready to dive in?

The Importance of Leadership in Today's World

Leadership Shapes Our World

Leadership is essential in shaping our world, from business organizations to social and political institutions. In the face of rapid technological advancements, globalization, and shifting societal values, the need for strong, effective, and adaptable leaders has never been greater. Why should you care about the importance of leadership in today's world? Because you may be a current or future leader, your decisions and impact will ripple outwards, affecting countless lives profoundly.

Addressing Complex Challenges

Today's leaders face unprecedented challenges, from climate change and political instability to wealth inequality and the future of work. These complex, intertwined issues demand innovative and collaborative solutions. Effective leaders have the power to inspire and mobilize people, organizations, and communities to tackle these problems head-on. As a reader seeking to master leadership skills, understanding the gravity of these challenges will help you appreciate your potential influence and the urgency of honing your leadership abilities.

The Power Of Inclusive Leadership

In today's increasingly diverse and interconnected world, the need for inclusive leadership has become paramount. Inclusive leaders embrace and leverage their team members' diverse perspectives and experiences to foster innovation and achieve better results. Emphasizing the importance of diversity and inclusion in leadership will help you understand the value of creating a culture where everyone feels valued, heard, and empowered to contribute. Are you ready to explore what being an effective and successful leader means?

Defining Effective and
Successful Leadership

What Makes A Leader Effective?

Effective leadership guides, inspires and influences others to achieve a common goal or vision. It involves skills, traits, and behaviors that enable leaders to adapt to changing circumstances, make sound decisions, and create environments where team members can thrive. But what exactly differentiates an effective leader from an ineffective one? And why should you care about these distinctions?

Essential Qualities Of Effective Leaders

There are several essential qualities and characteristics commonly associated with effective leadership. These include:

Self-awareness and emotional intelligence: Effective leaders possess a deep understanding of their emotions, strengths, weaknesses, and the impact of their actions on others. They can regulate their emotions and respond empathetically to the needs and concerns of their team members.

Vision and purpose: Effective leaders have a clear vision of what they want to achieve and can communicate this vision compellingly to their team. Despite setbacks and challenges, they demonstrate a strong sense of purpose and are committed to realizing their goals.

Adaptability and resilience: Effective leaders can adapt to changing circumstances, learn from mistakes, and bounce back from adversity. They are flexible and can pivot when necessary to overcome obstacles and achieve success.

Ethical behavior and integrity: Effective leaders are guided by a strong moral compass and act with integrity in all their dealings. They are honest, transparent, and accountable for their actions and decisions.

Empowerment and delegation: Effective leaders recognize the importance of empowering their team members and delegating tasks to leverage individual strengths. They trust their team to perform and provide the necessary support and resources to ensure success.

Understanding these qualities will help you to evaluate your leadership style and identify areas where you may need to grow and develop. So, how do you measure the success of a leader?

Defining Successful Leadership

Successful leadership consistently achieves desired outcomes while fostering a positive, collaborative, and growth-oriented environment. It goes beyond accomplishing goals and extends to a leader's long-term impact on their team, organization, and community. But what makes a leader successful, and why should you care about these success factors?

Indicators Of Successful Leadership

There are several indicators of successful leadership, which include:

High-performing teams: Successful leaders create high-performing teams with strong collaboration, open communication, and a shared commitment to achieving goals. These teams consistently deliver exceptional results and demonstrate high engagement and satisfaction.

Positive organizational culture: Successful leaders foster a positive culture where employees feel valued, supported, and motivated to contribute their best efforts. We characterize this culture by trusting each other, holding ourselves accountable, and focusing on continuous learning and improvement.

Adaptability and innovation: Successful leaders drive innovation and adaptability within their organization, embracing change and seeking new growth opportunities. They can identify emerging trends and challenges and pivot accordingly to ensure long-term success.

Long-lasting impact: Successful leaders leave a lasting legacy, whether through the development of their team members, the establishment of strong organizational values and practices, or the positive influence they have on the larger community.

Understanding these indicators of successful leadership will help you set clear benchmarks for your leadership journey and provide a roadmap for ongoing growth and development. With these definitions of effective and successful leadership in mind, are you ready to embark on the journey to mastering leadership skills?

The Journey to Mastering Leadership Skills

Developing A Growth Mindset

Cultivating a growth mindset - believing you can develop your abilities through dedication, effort, and feedback - is the first step in mastering leadership skills. This mindset enables you to view challenges as opportunities for growth and encourages you to seek out new experiences and learning opportunities continuously. Why should you care about developing a growth mindset? Because it will help you become a more resilient, adaptable, and effective leader better equipped to navigate the complexities of today's world.

Ongoing Learning And Reflection

Mastering leadership skills requires ongoing learning and reflection. To improve your leadership skills, seeking professional development opportunities, such as workshops, seminars, and mentorship programs, is essential. It also consists in regularly reflecting on your experiences, feedback from others, and your progress in developing critical leadership qualities. By committing yourself to continuous learning and reflection, you position yourself to grow as a leader and make a lasting impact on those around you. How can you develop effective and successful leaders' core traits and skills?

In the upcoming chapters, we will delve into effective leaders' core traits, communication, team building and management, decision-making and problem-solving skills, nurturing a results-oriented culture, leading through change and transformation, developing your leadership style, and balancing work and personal life. Each chapter will provide practical strategies, evidence-based insights, and real-life examples to guide your journey toward mastering the effective and successful leader mindset. Are you ready to take the first step and explore the core traits of effective leaders?

CHAPTER 2. THE CORE TRAITS OF EFFECTIVE LEADERS

Now that you understand the importance of leadership and the definitions of effective and successful leadership, it's time to explore the core traits that set exceptional leaders apart. This chapter will discuss six critical characteristics of effective leaders and provide evidence and examples to support these points. Are you ready to dive deeper and discover the essential qualities that will help you develop your leadership potential?

Self-Awareness and Emotional Intelligence

The Foundation Of Effective Leadership

Self-awareness and emotional intelligence form the foundation of effective leadership. Self-awareness is the ability to recognize and understand one's emotions, strengths, weaknesses, and the impact of one's actions on others. Emotional intelligence (EI) is the ability to perceive, understand, manage, and use emotions effectively in interpersonal relationships. But why should you care about developing self-awareness and emotional intelligence as a leader?

Enhanced Decision-Making And Communication

Research has shown that emotionally intelligent leaders make better decisions as they are more attuned to their emotions and can prevent emotional biases from clouding their judgment. Additionally, emotionally intelligent leaders are better communicators, as they can effectively tailor their message to their audience and convey their emotions. For example, when addressing a challenging situation, an emotionally intelligent leader can balance being assertive and empathetic, ensuring their message is well-received.

Stronger Relationships And Team Dynamics

Emotionally intelligent leaders also foster stronger relationships with their team members because they can better understand and manage their emotions and those of others. They can create a supportive and psychologically safe environment where team members feel comfortable sharing their thoughts and concerns. By doing so, they promote trust, collaboration, and a healthy team dynamic. Are you curious how having a clear vision and purpose can further enhance your leadership effectiveness?

Vision and Purpose

Guiding Your Team Towards A Shared Goal

A clear vision and purpose are essential for effective leadership, as it provides a roadmap for your team's efforts and helps guide decision-making. A strong vision outlines the desired future state of your organization or team and serves as a source of inspiration and motivation. Purpose, on the other hand, is the underlying reason or "why" behind your vision. But why should you care about developing a clear leadership vision and purpose?

Motivation And Engagement

Leaders who articulate a compelling vision and purpose inspire and motivate their team members to commit to a shared goal. A study by Bain & Company found that organizations with a strong sense of purpose are more likely to have engaged employees, who, in turn, are more productive and committed to their work. By aligning your team's efforts with a clear vision and purpose, you can create a sense of unity and focus that drives higher levels of performance and satisfaction. How can resilience and adaptability help you navigate the challenges of leadership?

Resilience and Adaptability

Navigating Challenges And Change

Resilience and adaptability are critical traits for effective leaders, especially in today's rapidly changing and uncertain world. Resilience is the ability to bounce back from adversity and maintain a sense of optimism and persistence in the face of challenges. Adaptability, on the other hand, refers to the ability to adjust and respond effectively to changing circumstances. Why should you care about developing resilience and adaptability as a leader?

Overcoming Obstacles And Achieving Success

Resilient and adaptable leaders are better equipped to overcome obstacles and succeed in challenging situations. Even when faced with difficult odds, they can maintain their composure and think creatively to find solutions. For example, consider the leadership of the late Steve Jobs, who was known for his ability to adapt and innovate in the face of setbacks and failures. Under his leadership, Apple Inc. survived numerous challenges and thrived, becoming one of the most valuable companies globally. By developing resilience and adaptability, you can lead your team through turbulent times and inspire them to succeed despite the odds. How do integrity and ethical behavior contribute to effective leadership?

Integrity and Ethical Behavior

The Cornerstone Of Trust And Respect

Integrity and ethical behavior are the cornerstones of trust and respect in leadership. Integrity involves consistently adhering to a set of moral and ethical principles, while ethical behavior encompasses acting in a manner that is honest, fair, and transparent. But why should you care about demonstrating integrity and ethical behavior as a leader?

Establishing Credibility And Long-Term Success

Leaders who exhibit integrity and ethical behavior establish credibility with their team members, peers, and stakeholders. They set the tone for ethical conduct within their organization and create an environment where employees feel confident that their leaders will make the right decisions. Moreover, research has shown that organizations with ethical leadership are more likely to achieve long-term success and avoid ethical scandals that can have severe financial and reputational consequences. By upholding the highest standards of integrity and ethical behavior, you will inspire trust and loyalty among your team members, ensuring your organization's long-term success. How can empathy and compassion elevate your leadership to new heights?

Empathy and Compassion

Connecting With Your Team On A Deeper Level

Empathy and compassion are essential traits for effective leaders, enabling you to connect with your team members on a deeper emotional level. Empathy is the ability to understand and share the feelings of others, while compassion is the willingness to help alleviate the suffering of others. But why should you care about developing empathy and compassion as a leader?

Enhanced Team Performance And Well-Being

Leaders who demonstrate empathy and compassion foster a supportive and inclusive environment where team members feel valued and understood. Research has shown that empathetic and compassionate leaders are likelier to engage and satisfy employees, improving team performance and well-being. Additionally, empathetic leaders are better equipped to handle conflict and mediate disputes among team members, as they can understand and validate the feelings and perspectives of all parties involved. You can create a positive, nurturing work environment that promotes collaboration, innovation, and success by cultivating empathy and compassion. How do humility and accountability factor into effective leadership?

Humility and Accountability

Recognizing Your Limitations And Owning Your

Actions

Humility and accountability are crucial traits for effective leaders, as they help maintain a balanced and grounded perspective on your leadership journey. Humility involves recognizing your limitations, valuing the input and expertise of others, and being open to learning and growth. On the other hand, accountability is the willingness to take responsibility for your actions and decisions, acknowledging and learning from your mistakes. But why should you care about developing humility and accountability as a leader?

Fostering A Culture Of Learning And Improvement

Humble and accountable leaders foster a culture of learning and improvement within their organization. By admitting their mistakes and taking responsibility for their actions, they set a powerful example for their team members and create an environment where learning, growing, and taking risks is safe. Research has shown that humble leaders are more likely to receive honest feedback from their team members and adapt their leadership style accordingly, leading to better team performance and outcomes. By embracing humility and accountability, you can create a learning-oriented culture that drives continuous improvement, innovation, and success.

As you continue on your journey to becoming an effective and successful leader, reflect on these core traits and consider how you can integrate them into your leadership style. Are you ready to delve into the art of communication and learn how mastering this essential skill can further enhance your leadership effectiveness?

In the following chapters, we will explore other critical aspects of leadership, such as the art of communication, team building and management, decision-making and problem-solving skills, nurturing a results-oriented culture, leading through change and transformation, developing your leadership style, and balancing work and personal life. By gaining a deeper understanding of these topics and applying the practical strategies and evidence-based insights provided, you will be well on your way to mastering the effective and successful leader mindset. Are you excited to continue your leadership journey and discover the secrets to becoming an exceptional communicator?

CHAPTER 3. THE ART OF COMMUNICATION

A s an aspiring effective, and successful leader, mastering the art of communication is a vital skill to develop. Effective communication builds the foundation for relationships, facilitates the sharing of ideas, and helps achieve goals. In this chapter, we will explore four critical aspects of communication and provide evidence and examples to support their importance in effective leadership. Are you ready to unlock the secrets of exceptional communication and enhance your leadership potential?

The Power of Active Listening

Creating A Strong Foundation For Communication

Active listening is a critical component of effective communication and is the foundation for strong interpersonal relationships. Active listening involves fully focusing on, understanding, and responding to the speaker, providing feedback, and demonstrating genuine interest in their message. But why should you care about developing active listening skills as a leader?

Improved Team Dynamics And Decision-Making

Active listening can lead to improved team dynamics and better decision-making. When leaders actively listen to their team members, they create an environment where everyone feels heard and valued. Active listening can increase trust, collaboration, and a sense of psychological safety within the team. Additionally, by actively listening to diverse perspectives, leaders are more likely to make well-informed decisions considering all stakeholders' needs and concerns. How can delivering constructive feedback further enhance your communication skills?

Delivering Constructive Feedback

Fostering Growth And Improvement

Constructive feedback is essential for fostering growth and improvement in your team members. It involves providing specific, actionable, and timely information that helps individuals identify areas for development and recognize their strengths. But why should you care about delivering constructive feedback as a leader?

Increased Performance And Engagement

Research has shown that employees who receive regular, constructive feedback are more likely to be engaged, satisfied, and high-performing. By providing clear and actionable feedback, leaders help their team members understand their performance expectations, identify areas for improvement, and recognize their achievements. As a result, team members may experience increased motivation, commitment, and overall performance. Are you ready to discover how storytelling can inspire and motivate your team?

Storytelling for Inspiration and Motivation

Connecting With Your Team On An Emotional Level

Storytelling is a powerful tool for leaders to connect with their team on an emotional level, inspire, and motivate them. Leaders can create a memorable and lasting impact on their team members by sharing personal experiences and lessons learned or conveying a message through a relatable story. But why should you care about mastering the art of storytelling as a leader?

Influencing And Persuading Your Team

Storytelling can influence and persuade your team, allowing you to appeal to their emotions, values, and beliefs. Research has shown that stories can be more persuasive than facts and figures, engaging the listener's emotions, imagination, and cognitive faculties. By incorporating storytelling into your communication repertoire, you can inspire your team to embrace new ideas, overcome challenges, and work towards a shared vision. How can nonverbal communication further enhance your ability to connect with your team?

Mastering Nonverbal Communication

Communicating Beyond Words

Nonverbal communication is an essential aspect of effective communication that involves conveying messages through facial expressions, gestures, body language, tone of voice, and eye contact. Research suggests that nonverbal cues can account for up to 93% of the overall meaning in face-to-face communication. But why should you care about mastering nonverbal communication as a leader?

Enhancing Clarity And Reducing Misunderstandings

Nonverbal cues can significantly enhance the clarity of your message and reduce the likelihood of misunderstandings. For example, maintaining eye contact while speaking can convey confidence and sincerity, while adopting an open posture can signal receptiveness and approachability. By being mindful of your nonverbal cues, you can ensure that your team members effectively communicate and understand your intended message.

Building Trust And Rapport

Effective nonverbal communication can also help build trust and rapport with your team members. You can demonstrate empathy and establish a stronger connection with your team by displaying positive nonverbal cues such as nodding in agreement, maintaining an open posture, and mirroring the body language of others. Active listening skills can increase your team's trust, respect, and collaboration.

Detecting And Addressing Hidden Concerns

Mastering nonverbal communication can also help you detect and address hidden concerns within your team. By observing and interpreting nonverbal cues, you can identify potential issues or conflicts that people may not explicitly express through words. For example, if a team member avoids eye contact or displays closed body language during a meeting, it could indicate discomfort, disagreement, or a lack of understanding. By addressing these concerns proactively, you can create a more open and supportive environment that fosters effective communication and collaboration.

As you continue on your journey to mastering the effective and successful leader mindset, take the time to develop and refine your communication skills. Reflect on the importance of active listening, delivering constructive feedback, storytelling, and nonverbal communication in your leadership practice. Doing so will enhance your ability to connect with, inspire, and motivate your team members, ultimately leading to greater success and satisfaction in your leadership role.

Are you eager to learn more about team building and management and how these skills can contribute to your growth as an effective and successful leader? In the next chapter, we will delve into the intricacies of team building and management, exploring essential strategies and techniques for fostering a high-performing, collaborative, and engaged team.

CHAPTER 4. TEAM BUILDING AND MANAGEMENT

A s an effective and successful leader, your ability to build, manage, and inspire high-performing teams is crucial. A cohesive team can achieve significant results, foster innovation, and contribute to a healthy organizational culture. This chapter will explore five critical aspects of team building and management, providing evidence and examples to support their importance in effective leadership. Are you ready to take your team to new heights by mastering these essential skills?

Identifying and Leveraging
Individual Strengths

Capitalizing On The Diversity Of Your Team

One of the most critical aspects of team building and management is identifying and leveraging the individual strengths of your team members. Each person brings unique skills, experiences, and perspectives to the table. But why should you care about recognizing and capitalizing on the diverse strengths within your team?

Increased Performance And Innovation

Research has shown that teams with diverse skill sets and strengths are likelier to perform at higher levels and generate innovative ideas. By identifying the unique strengths of each team member and assigning tasks that align with their skills, you can optimize their performance and job satisfaction. This approach also fosters a sense of ownership and commitment to the team's objectives. How can you create a collaborative, inclusive environment maximizing your team's potential?

*Creating a Collaborative and
Inclusive Environment*

Fostering A Culture Of Trust And Respect

Creating a collaborative and inclusive environment is essential for your team's success. To achieve this, you must foster a culture of trust and respect where all team members feel valued and included and their contributions are recognized. But why should you care about cultivating a collaborative and inclusive environment as a leader?

Enhanced Team Performance And Employee Engagement

Teams operating within a collaborative and inclusive environment are likelier to have higher performance levels, creativity, and employee engagement. Research has shown that when team members feel included and valued, they are more likely to share their ideas, take risks, and contribute to their success. Moreover, an inclusive environment promotes psychological safety, which high-performing teams identify as critical. Are you prepared to navigate the challenges of conflict resolution and mediation within your team?

Conflict Resolution and Mediation

Managing Disagreements And Resolving Issues

Conflict resolution and mediation involve addressing disputes, facilitating open communication, and working toward mutually satisfactory solutions. Conflict is inevitable in any team, and your ability to effectively manage disagreements and resolve issues is crucial as a leader. But why should you care about developing conflict resolution and mediation skills as a leader?

Maintaining Team Cohesion And Productivity

Conflict resolution and mediation can help maintain team cohesion, productivity, and morale. You can prevent issues from escalating and negatively impacting the team's performance by addressing conflicts proactively and constructively. Moreover, conflict resolution can improve understanding, trust, and collaboration among team members, ultimately contributing to a healthier team dynamic. Are you ready to explore the art of delegation and empowerment and how it can benefit your team?

Delegation and Empowerment

Maximizing Your Team's Potential

Delegation and empowerment are essential skills for effective team management. Delegation involves assigning tasks and responsibilities to team members, while empowerment means giving them the autonomy, resources, and support they need to succeed. But why should you care about delegating and empowering your team members as a leader?

Increased Efficiency, Development, And Motivation

Delegation and empowerment can increase team members' efficiency, professional development, and motivation. By delegating tasks and empowering team members, you free up time to focus on higher-level strategic activities while providing growth and skill development opportunities. Research has shown that empowered employees are more likely to be engaged, committed, and high-performing. Furthermore, delegation and empowerment can increase job satisfaction and a sense of ownership among team members, ultimately contributing to the team's overall success. How can fostering a growth mindset within your team further enhance its performance and success?

Fostering a Growth Mindset
within the Team

Promoting A Culture Of Continuous Learning And Development

A growth mindset is a belief that you can develop your abilities and intelligence through effort, persistence, and the right learning strategies. Fostering a growth mindset within your team involves promoting a culture of continuous learning, development, and adaptability. But why should you care about nurturing a growth mindset in your team as a leader?

Increased Adaptability And Performance

Research has shown that teams with a growth mindset are more adaptable, resilient, and high-performing. When faced with challenges, they are more likely to see them as opportunities for growth rather than threats. Moreover, when team members embrace feedback, learn from failures, and continually seek improvement, they cultivate a growth mindset. A growth mindset can lead to increased innovation, problem-solving capabilities, and overall performance within the team.

Mastering the skills of team building and management is essential for effective and successful leadership. By identifying and leveraging individual strengths, creating a collaborative and inclusive environment, resolving conflicts, delegating and empowering your team, and fostering a growth mindset, you can unlock your team's full potential and drive its success. As you continue your leadership journey, reflect on these essential aspects of team building and management, and strive to implement them in your practice.

Are you ready to delve deeper into critical decision-making and problem-solving skills and discover how they can enhance your leadership effectiveness? The next chapter will explore various decision-making and problem-solving strategies, providing evidence and examples to support their importance in effective leadership.

CHAPTER 5. DECISION-MAKING AND PROBLEM-SOLVING SKILLS

Y our ability to make sound decisions and solve complex problems is crucial as an effective and successful leader. These skills significantly affect your team's success and can ultimately impact your organization's performance. This chapter will explore four critical aspects of decision-making and problem-solving, providing evidence and examples to support their importance in effective leadership. Are you ready to hone your decision-making and problem-solving abilities to become a more effective leader?

*Understanding Different
Decision-Making Styles*

Adapting To Various Situations And Team Dynamics

As a leader, understanding different decision-making styles can help you adapt to various situations and team dynamics. Decision-making styles can range from autocratic, where the leader makes decisions without input from others, to participative, where the leader involves team members in decision-making. But why should you care about understanding and adapting your leadership decision-making style?

Increased Team Satisfaction And Performance

Research has shown that aligning your decision-making style with the needs of your team and the situation at hand can lead to increased team satisfaction and performance. For example, a participative approach may be more effective when team members possess valuable expertise or when building consensus is essential. By understanding and adapting your decision-making style, you can make better-informed decisions considering each situation's unique context and requirements. Are you prepared to enhance your analytical thinking and critical evaluation skills to improve your decision-making abilities?

Analytical Thinking and
Critical Evaluation

Making Informed And Well-Reasoned Decisions

Analytical thinking and critical evaluation are essential for making informed and well-reasoned decisions. Analytical thinking involves breaking down complex information into smaller, more manageable parts, while critical evaluation requires assessing the information's validity, reliability, and relevance to make an informed decision. But why should you care about developing your analytical thinking and critical evaluation skills as a leader?

Increased Decision Quality And Reduced Bias

By employing analytical thinking and critical evaluation, you can improve the quality of your decisions and reduce the impact of biases and errors. This approach allows you to weigh the pros and cons of various options, consider alternative perspectives, and assess the potential consequences of your decisions. Making well-reasoned and evidence-based decisions can enhance your credibility as a leader and increase the likelihood of successful outcomes for your team and organization. How can managing risk and uncertainty further strengthen your decision-making abilities?

Managing Risk and Uncertainty

Navigating Complex And Ambiguous Situations

Managing risk and uncertainty is critical for effective decision-making and problem-solving, especially in today's fast-paced and dynamic business environment. Leaders must be able to navigate complex and ambiguous situations, assess potential risks, and make decisions despite incomplete or uncertain information. But why should you care about developing your ability to manage risk and uncertainty as a leader?

Enhanced Resilience And Adaptability

By effectively managing risk and uncertainty, you can enhance your team's resilience and adaptability, ensuring its success in the face of change and unforeseen challenges. This skill enables you to identify potential threats and opportunities, develop contingency plans, and make proactive decisions to mitigate risks and capitalize on opportunities. As a result, your team will be better equipped to navigate uncertainty, adapt to change, and maintain high-performance levels. Are you eager to explore how creativity and innovation can improve your problem-solving abilities?

Creativity and Innovation in Problem-Solving

Generating Novel Solutions To Complex Challenges

Creativity and innovation are essential for generating novel solutions to complex challenges and driving continuous improvement within your team and organization. Creative problem-solving involves thinking outside the box, challenging assumptions, and exploring new ideas and approaches. But why should you care about nurturing creativity and innovation in your problem-solving efforts as a leader?

Increased Competitive Advantage And Adaptability

You can enhance your team's competitive advantage and adaptability by fostering creativity and innovation in problem-solving. Teams that consistently generate novel solutions are more likely to stay ahead of the competition, capitalize on new opportunities, and overcome challenges in a rapidly changing business landscape. Moreover, creative problem-solving can improve processes, products, and services, contributing to your organization's overall success.

Promoting A Culture Of Innovation

As a leader, promoting a culture of innovation within your

team is essential, encouraging team members to share their ideas, experiment with new approaches, and learn from failure. Leaders can create an environment where innovation thrives by encouraging creativity and empowering team members to take risks and push boundaries. As a result, team members are more likely to feel engaged and motivated and perform better.

Mastering decision-making and problem-solving skills are essential for effective and successful leadership. By understanding different decision-making styles, enhancing your analytical thinking and critical evaluation abilities, managing risk and uncertainty, and fostering creativity and innovation, you can make better-informed decisions and solve complex problems more effectively. As you continue your leadership journey, reflect on these essential skills and strive to incorporate them into your practice.

Are you ready to explore the importance of continuous learning and professional development and discover how these pursuits can contribute to your growth as an effective and successful leader? In the next chapter, we will delve into the intricacies of lifelong learning, exploring essential strategies and techniques for fostering personal and professional growth.

CHAPTER 6.
NURTURING A RESULTS-ORIENTED CULTURE

A s an effective and successful leader, fostering a results-oriented culture within your team is vital for driving performance, growth, and success. A results-oriented culture emphasizes the achievement of goals, continuous improvement, and the pursuit of excellence. This chapter will explore four critical aspects of nurturing a results-oriented culture, providing evidence and examples to support their importance in effective leadership. Are you ready to learn how to create an environment where your team thrives and consistently delivers outstanding results?

Setting SMART Goals and Objectives

Establishing Clear And Achievable Targets

Setting SMART goals and objectives is the foundation of a results-oriented culture. Establishing clear and achievable targets gives your team a roadmap for success and a sense of direction. SMART goals are Specific, Measurable, Achievable, Relevant, and Time-bound. But why should you care about setting SMART goals and objectives as a leader?

Increased Focus, Motivation, And Performance

Research has shown that SMART goals can increase team members' focus, motivation, and performance. When goals are specific and measurable, team members better understand their expectations and can allocate their time and resources effectively. Achievable and relevant goals provide a sense of purpose, while time-bound goals create a sense of urgency, driving team members to act decisively and efficiently. How can measuring performance and tracking progress contribute to a results-oriented culture?

Measuring Performance and
Tracking Progress

Evaluating Success And Identifying Areas For Improvement

Measuring performance and tracking progress are essential for evaluating the success of your team's efforts and identifying areas for improvement. Regularly assessing your team's performance against established goals and objectives ensures that your team stays on track and focuses on delivering results. But why should you care about measuring performance and tracking progress as a leader?

Enhanced Accountability And Continuous Improvement

By monitoring performance and progress, you can enhance accountability within your team and foster a culture of continuous improvement. Regular performance evaluations and progress updates enable team members to understand their contributions to the team's success and identify areas where they can improve. As a result, team members may become more motivated, engaged, and better equipped to perform their roles effectively. Are you prepared to explore how recognizing and rewarding achievements can strengthen your results-oriented culture?

Recognizing and Rewarding Achievements

Motivating And Engaging Your Team

Recognizing and rewarding achievements are crucial for motivating and engaging your team in a results-oriented culture. Acknowledging your team members' accomplishments and hard work demonstrates that you value their contributions and reinforce their commitment to achieving goals. But why should you care about recognizing and rewarding achievements as a leader?

Increased Job Satisfaction And Retention

Research has shown that recognition and rewards can increase team members' job satisfaction, performance, and retention. By celebrating successes, large and small, you create a positive work environment where team members feel appreciated and motivated to continue delivering exceptional results. Furthermore, a well-structured rewards system can incentivize team members to push themselves and strive for excellence. How can embracing failure and learning from mistakes contribute to a results-oriented culture?

Embracing Failure and
Learning from Mistakes

Promoting A Growth Mindset And Continuous Improvement

Embracing failure and learning from mistakes is essential to nurturing a results-oriented culture. By acknowledging that failure is a natural part of the learning process, you promote a growth mindset and encourage continuous improvement within your team. But why should you care about embracing failure and learning from mistakes as a leader?

Increased Innovation And Resilience

By fostering an environment where team members feel comfortable taking risks and learning from their failures, you can increase innovation and resilience within your team. When team members are not afraid to fail, they are more likely to explore new ideas, experiment with different approaches, and push the boundaries of what is possible. This mindset can lead to developing novel solutions and strategies, ultimately enhancing your team's competitive advantage.

Cultivating Psychological Safety And Trust

Additionally, embracing failure and learning from mistakes can help cultivate psychological safety and trust within your team. When team members feel that their leader is supportive and understanding in the face of failure, they are more likely to share their concerns, ideas, and challenges openly. This transparency can lead to more effective collaboration, problem-solving, and decision-making, further contributing to your team's success.

Nurturing a results-oriented culture is essential for effective and successful leadership. By setting SMART goals and objectives, measuring performance and tracking progress, recognizing and rewarding achievements, and embracing failure and learning from mistakes, you can create an environment where your team thrives and consistently delivers outstanding results. As you continue your leadership journey, reflect on these essential strategies and strive to incorporate them into your practice.

Are you ready to explore the importance of self-care and work-life balance and discover how these pursuits can contribute to your effectiveness as a leader? In the next chapter, we will delve into the intricacies of maintaining a healthy balance between personal and professional responsibilities, exploring essential strategies and techniques for promoting well-being and sustainable success.

CHAPTER 7.
LEADING THROUGH CHANGE AND TRANSFORMATION

C hange is inevitable, and organizations must continuously adapt to remain competitive and achieve sustainable growth. In today's rapidly evolving business landscape, the ability to lead through change and transformation is a critical skill for effective and successful leaders. This chapter will explore four key aspects of leading through change and transformation, providing evidence and examples to support their importance in effective leadership. Are you ready to learn how to navigate the complexities of change management and become a catalyst for positive organizational transformation?

The Dynamics of Change Management

Understanding The Change Process

The first step in leading through change and transformation

is understanding the dynamics of change management. Change management involves the process of planning, implementing, and sustaining organizational change while minimizing disruptions and maximizing the benefits. But why should you care about the dynamics of change management as a leader?

Increased Efficiency And Success Rate

By understanding the change management process, you can increase the efficiency and success rate of change initiatives within your organization. You can help your team prepare for changes, understand the reasons, and commit to making the necessary adjustments by executing a change management strategy effectively. Implementing an effective change management strategy can lead to improved performance, reduced resistance, and increased buy-in from team members. How can successfully overcoming resistance to change enhance your success as a leader?

Overcoming Resistance to Change

Addressing Concerns And Misconceptions

Resistance to change is a natural human response, as change often brings uncertainty, fear, and potential loss of control. As a leader, it is crucial to overcome resistance to change by addressing concerns and misconceptions and involving team members in the change process. But why should you care about overcoming resistance to change as a leader?

Enhanced Adoption And Adaptability

By addressing resistance to change and involving team members in the change process, leaders can enhance the adoption and adaptability of their team. This approach can lead to a smoother transition, reduced disruptions, and more successful change initiative implementation. Moreover, by actively involving team members in the change process, you can promote a sense of ownership and commitment, improving morale and performance during the transition. Are you prepared to explore the role of leadership in organizational transformation?

Leading Organizational Transformation

Inspiring And Guiding Your Team

Leading organizational transformation involves inspiring and guiding your team through significant changes that affect the entire organization. As a leader, you are responsible for inspiring and guiding your team through significant changes that affect the organization, such as mergers and acquisitions, restructuring, or implementing new strategies, processes, or technologies. But why should you care about leading organizational transformation as a leader?

Ensuring Long-Term Success And Sustainability

You can ensure your organization's long-term success and sustainability by effectively leading organizational transformation. Successful transformations can lead to increased efficiency, competitiveness, and growth. Furthermore, by inspiring and guiding your team through the transformation process, you can foster a sense of unity and shared purpose, increasing team engagement, motivation, and performance. How can fostering a culture of continuous improvement further enhance your ability to lead through change and transformation?

Fostering a Culture of Continuous Improvement

Encouraging Ongoing Learning And Growth

Fostering a culture of continuous improvement involves encouraging ongoing learning, growth, and innovation within your organization. By promoting a mindset that values experimentation, learning from mistakes, and embracing new ideas, you can create an environment where your team consistently seeks opportunities for improvement and adaptation. But why should you care about fostering a culture of continuous improvement as a leader?

Increased Innovation And Competitive Advantage

By nurturing a culture of continuous improvement, you can increase innovation and create a competitive advantage for your organization. Teams that consistently strive for improvement are more likely to stay ahead of the competition, capitalize on new opportunities, and adapt to the ever-changing business landscape. Consistent effort toward improvement can lead to sustained growth, profitability, and success for your organization.

Enhanced Resilience And Adaptability

Furthermore, a continuous improvement culture can enhance your team's resilience and adaptability. Team members who regularly evaluate processes, learn from their mistakes, and embrace new ideas are better equipped to navigate change and uncertainty. This agility can enable your organization to respond more effectively to shifts in the market or industry.

Leading through change and transformation is essential for effective and successful leaders. By understanding the dynamics of change management, overcoming resistance to change, leading organizational transformation, and fostering a culture of continuous improvement, you can navigate the complexities of change and become a catalyst for positive transformation within your organization. As you continue your leadership journey, reflect on these critical strategies and strive to incorporate them into your practice.

Are you ready to explore the importance of personal development and continuous learning in your leadership journey? In the next chapter, we will explore the essential strategies and techniques for promoting your growth and development as a leader, ensuring you are always prepared to meet the challenges and opportunities.

CHAPTER 8. DEVELOPING YOUR PERSONAL LEADERSHIP STYLE

Developing your leadership style is crucial as you progress on your journey to mastering the effective and successful leader mindset. Your unique style will define how you interact with your team, approach challenges, and make decisions. This chapter will explore four critical aspects of developing your leadership style, providing evidence and examples to support their importance in effective leadership. Are you ready to learn how to identify your strengths and weaknesses, build a personal leadership philosophy, embrace a lifelong learning mindset, and seek mentorship and networking opportunities?

Assessing Your Strengths and Weaknesses

Self-Reflection And Self-Assessment

The first step in developing your leadership style is assessing your strengths and weaknesses. You must first evaluate your strengths and weaknesses to develop your leadership style. Self-reflection and self-assessment can help you better understand your unique leadership skills, traits, and characteristics. But why should you consider assessing your strengths and weaknesses as a leader?

Targeted Improvement And Leveraging Strengths

By identifying your strengths and weaknesses as a leader, you can engage in targeted improvement to address areas where you may need to grow or develop. This targeted improvement can lead to increased leadership effectiveness and a greater ability to inspire and motivate your team. Moreover, by recognizing your strengths, you can leverage them to your advantage, capitalizing on your unique talents and abilities to drive success within your organization. How can building a personal leadership philosophy contribute to your personal leadership style?

*Building a Personal
Leadership Philosophy*

Defining Your Core Values And Beliefs

Building a personal leadership philosophy involves defining your core values and beliefs, which will guide your actions, decisions, and interactions as a leader. Your leadership philosophy should reflect who you are and what you stand for, providing a foundation for your leadership style. But why should you care about building a personal leadership philosophy as a leader?

Consistency, Trust, And Credibility

By establishing a personal leadership philosophy, you can create consistency in your actions and decision-making, increasing trust and credibility among your team members. When your team understands your core values and beliefs, they are more likely to feel secure and supported, fostering a positive work environment where they can thrive. Furthermore, a well-defined leadership philosophy can serve as a guide during times of uncertainty or change, helping you stay true to your principles and navigate challenging situations with confidence. How can embracing a lifelong learning mindset enhance your leadership style?

Embracing a Lifelong Learning Mindset

Continuous Growth And Development

Embracing a lifelong learning mindset involves committing to continuous growth and development as a leader. Actively seeking opportunities to expand knowledge, skills, and perspectives, remaining open to new ideas, and adapting leadership styles as needed means committing to continuous growth and development as a leader. But why should you care about embracing a lifelong learning mindset as a leader?

Staying Ahead And Adapting To Change

As industries and markets evolve, leaders committed to learning and growth are better positioned to respond to new challenges, capitalize on emerging opportunities, and lead their teams through periods of change and transformation. By adopting a lifelong learning mindset, you can stay ahead of the curve and adapt to the ever-changing business landscape. Furthermore, continually developing your skills and knowledge can enhance your leadership effectiveness and inspire your team to do the same. How can seeking mentorship and networking opportunities contribute to your leadership style?

Seeking Mentorship and Networking Opportunities

Learning From Experienced Leaders

Seeking mentorship and networking opportunities involves connecting with experienced leaders who can offer guidance, support, and insights into your leadership journey. By engaging with mentors and networking with other professionals, you can access valuable advice, resources, and perspectives that can inform your leadership style and help you grow as a leader. But why should you care about seeking mentorship and networking opportunities as a leader?

Expanding Your Perspectives And Accelerating Growth

By engaging with mentors and networking with other professionals, leaders can expand their perspectives, challenge their assumptions, and learn from the experiences and insights of others. This experience can accelerate personal and professional growth, enabling them to become more effective and successful leaders. Moreover, these relationships can provide a support system, helping you navigate the challenges and uncertainties that inevitably arise during your leadership journey.

Opening Doors To New Opportunities

Additionally, mentorship and networking can open new

opportunities, such as job offers, collaborations, or partnerships. These opportunities can provide valuable experience and contribute to your leadership growth and development. Furthermore, by expanding your network, you increase your visibility and credibility within your industry, which can lead to further opportunities and career advancement.

Developing your leadership style is critical to mastering an effective and successful leadership mindset. By assessing your strengths and weaknesses, building a personal leadership philosophy, embracing a lifelong learning mindset, and seeking mentorship and networking opportunities, you can cultivate a unique leadership style that drives success within your organization and inspires your team to excel. As you continue your leadership journey, reflect on these critical strategies and strive to incorporate them into your practice.

Are you ready to explore the importance of maintaining a healthy work-life balance and prioritizing self-care as a leader? In the next chapter, we will delve into the essential strategies and techniques for managing stress, maintaining balance, and ensuring that you can sustain your effectiveness and well-being as a leader in the long term.

CHAPTER 9.
BALANCING WORK
AND PERSONAL LIFE

As you strive to master the effective and successful leader mindset, it's crucial to consider balancing your work and personal life. Maintaining a healthy balance can contribute significantly to your overall well-being and effectiveness as a leader. This chapter will explore four critical aspects of balancing work and personal life: managing stress and avoiding burnout, practicing mindfulness and emotional regulation, cultivating work-life harmony for personal growth, and role-modeling healthy boundaries for your team. Are you ready to learn to maintain a healthy work-life balance and prioritize self-care?

Managing Stress and
Avoiding Burnout

Recognizing The Impact Of Stress On Leadership

The first step in balancing work and personal life is managing stress and avoiding burnout. As a leader, you face numerous challenges and pressures that can lead to high-stress levels if not managed effectively. But why should you care about managing stress and avoiding burnout as a leader?

Sustained Effectiveness And Well-Being

Managing stress and avoiding burnout is essential for maintaining your effectiveness and well-being as a leader. Prolonged stress can result in decreased productivity, impaired decision-making, and diminished emotional intelligence. Moreover, chronic stress can lead to burnout, a state of emotional, physical, and mental exhaustion that can adversely affect your personal and professional life. By learning to manage stress and avoid burnout, you can sustain your effectiveness as a leader and ensure that you can support and inspire your team over the long term. How can practicing mindfulness and emotional regulation contribute to a healthy work-life balance?

Practicing Mindfulness and Emotional Regulation

The Benefits Of Mindfulness For Leaders

Practicing mindfulness and emotional regulation is critical to balancing work and personal life as a leader. Mindfulness involves paying attention to your thoughts, feelings, and bodily sensations in the present moment without judgment. Emotional regulation refers to managing and modulating your emotions in response to various situations. But why should you care about practicing mindfulness and emotional regulation as a leader?

Enhanced Focus, Resilience, And Empathy

Practicing mindfulness and emotional regulation can provide numerous benefits for leaders, including enhanced focus, increased resilience, and improved empathy. Mindfulness can help you stay present and engaged in your work, allowing you to manage stress better and maintain your effectiveness as a leader. Emotional regulation can contribute to your ability to navigate challenging situations with grace and maintain positive relationships with your team. Furthermore, mindfulness and emotional regulation can enhance empathy, enabling you to understand better and support your team members. How can cultivating work-life harmony for personal growth support a healthy work-life balance?

Cultivating Work-Life Harmony for Personal Growth

Redefining The Concept Of Balance

Cultivating work-life harmony for personal growth involves redefining the concept of balance and recognizing that your personal and professional lives are interconnected. Instead of striving for a rigid separation between work and personal life, consider how you can create harmony between the various aspects of your life, ensuring that they complement and support one another. But why should you care about cultivating work-life balance for personal growth as a leader?

Increased Satisfaction And Overall Well-Being

By embracing the concept of work-life harmony, you can experience increased satisfaction and overall well-being in your personal and professional lives. When you view your work and personal life as interconnected, you can prioritize your time and energy more effectively, ensuring you can devote adequate attention to the activities and relationships that matter most to you. This prioritization can result in a more fulfilling and rewarding life and increased leadership effectiveness and success. How can role modeling healthy boundaries for your team contribute to a healthy work-life balance?

Role Modeling Healthy Boundaries for Your Team

Demonstrating The Importance Of Boundaries

As a leader, you are responsible and can model healthy boundaries for your team. By setting and maintaining clear boundaries between your work and personal life, you can demonstrate the importance of prioritizing self-care and maintaining a healthy work-life balance. But why should you care about role modeling healthy boundaries for your team as a leader?

Promoting A Healthy Work Environment And Employee Well-Being

Role modeling healthy boundaries can contribute to a healthier work environment and support the well-being of your team members. When you prioritize self-care and maintain a healthy work-life balance, you encourage your team to do the same. Encouraging team members to prioritize self-care and maintain a healthy work-life balance can increase job satisfaction, decrease stress, and improve overall well-being. Furthermore, promoting a healthy work environment can enhance your team's productivity, engagement, and organizational commitment.

Encouraging Sustainable Success

A healthy work-life balance enables you and your team to maintain your effectiveness and well-being over the long term, supporting the ongoing success of your organization. You can also encourage sustainable success within your team and organization by role-modeling healthy boundaries. Fostering a culture that values work-life balance can help your organization attract and retain top talent, further contributing to its success.

Balancing work and personal life is critical to mastering an effective and successful leadership mindset. By managing stress and avoiding burnout, practicing mindfulness and emotional regulation, cultivating work-life harmony for personal growth, and role-modeling healthy boundaries for your team, you can maintain a healthy work-life balance and ensure that you can sustain your effectiveness and well-being as a leader. As you continue your leadership journey, reflect on these critical strategies and strive to incorporate them into your practice.

Are you prepared to put your newfound knowledge into action and make a lasting impact on your organization and team? In the next chapter, we will explore strategies for implementing the concepts and practices discussed in this book, ensuring that you can successfully apply the principles of effective and successful leadership to your unique context and circumstances.

CHAPTER 10.
BECOMING A
MASTERFUL LEADER:
A RECAP AND
NEXT STEPS

Throughout this book, we have explored various aspects of mastering the effective and successful leader mindset, including developing core traits, honing communication skills, building, and managing teams, fostering decision-making and problem-solving skills, nurturing a results-oriented culture, leading through change and transformation, and cultivating a personal leadership style. In this concluding chapter, we will reflect on the journey of leadership mastery, consider the potential for becoming a force for positive change, and discuss the lasting impact of effective and successful leadership. Are you ready to embrace the journey of leadership mastery and create a lasting effect on your organization and beyond?

*Embracing the Journey of
Leadership Mastery*

Leadership As A Continuous Learning Process

One key theme that emerged throughout this book is the idea that leadership is a continuous learning process. As you strive to master the effective and successful leader mindset, it is essential to remember that the journey of leadership mastery is ongoing. But why should you care about embracing the journey of leadership mastery as a leader?

Adaptability And Growth In A Changing World

Embracing the journey of leadership mastery ensures that you remain adaptable and continue to grow as a leader in a constantly changing world. By committing to ongoing learning and development, you can stay abreast of new trends, challenges, and opportunities, ensuring you can navigate the complexities of the modern business landscape effectively. Moreover, by embracing the journey of leadership mastery, you can inspire your team to do the same, fostering a culture of continuous improvement and growth. How can being a force for positive change contribute to your leadership success?

Becoming a Force for Positive Change

The Power Of Effective And Successful Leadership

As you strive to master the effective and successful leader mindset, you have the potential to become a force for positive change within your organization and beyond. By embodying the core traits and principles discussed throughout this book, you can inspire, empower, and support your team to achieve their full potential, drive innovation and growth, and make a meaningful impact in the world. But why should you care about becoming a force for positive change as a leader?

Creating A Legacy Of Success And Impact

Becoming a force for positive change can contribute to your success and legacy as a leader. When you prioritize the well-being and development of your team, lead with integrity and empathy, and drive positive change within your organization and industry, you create a lasting impact that transcends your accomplishments. Moreover, you can contribute to your organization's long-term success and sustainability by fostering a culture of innovation, collaboration, and continuous improvement. How can the lasting impact of effective and successful leadership benefit your organization and team?

The Lasting Impact of Effective
and Successful Leadership

Inspiring Future Generations Of Leaders

One of the most significant aspects of effective and successful leadership is its lasting impact on your organization, team, and future generations of leaders. Embodying the principles and practices discussed in this book, you can create a ripple effect beyond your immediate sphere of influence. But why should you care about the lasting impact of effective and successful leadership as a leader?

Building A Sustainable And Resilient Organization

The lasting impact of effective and successful leadership can contribute to the development of a sustainable and resilient organization. When you prioritize the well-being and growth of your team, lead with integrity and empathy, and foster a culture of innovation and continuous improvement, you create a strong foundation for the ongoing success of your organization. Moreover, by inspiring future generations of leaders, you can help ensure that your organization remains adaptable and resilient in the face of change and uncertainty.

Creating A Better World Through Leadership

Finally, the lasting impact of effective and successful leadership can contribute to creating a better world through your influence and the positive changes you inspire within your organization and industry. By prioritizing ethical behavior, social responsibility, and environmental sustainability, you can help address pressing global challenges and create a brighter future for all.

The journey of leadership mastery is an ongoing process that requires continuous learning, growth, and development. By embracing this journey and striving to become a force for positive change, you can create a lasting impact on your organization, your team, and the world at large. As you progress in your leadership journey, we encourage you to reflect on the principles and practices discussed in this book and commit to embodying the effective and successful leader mindset in all aspects of your life.

As you conclude your exploration of mastering the effective and successful leader mindset, consider the following question: Are you ready to apply the concepts, strategies, and practices discussed in this book to your unique context and circumstances and make a lasting impact as a leader? Doing so will contribute to your organization's success, your team's well-being, and the creation of a better world through effective and successful leadership.

The Importance Of Mentoring And Giving Back

As you continue your journey of leadership mastery, it's important to remember the role that mentorship and giving back can play in your development. Mentors can provide valuable guidance, support, and feedback, helping you navigate leadership challenges and opportunities more confidently and effectively. And by giving back, whether through volunteering, mentoring others, or supporting causes that align with your values, you can positively impact those around you and contribute to a better world.

The Power Of Mindset

Finally, we must recognize the incredible power of mindset in shaping our experiences and outcomes as leaders. Our beliefs about ourselves, our abilities, and our potential can profoundly impact our success and fulfillment as leaders. By cultivating a growth mindset, embracing failure and setbacks as opportunities for learning and growth, and approaching our journey of leadership mastery with curiosity, humility, and resilience, we can tap into our full potential and make a meaningful difference in the world.

As you close this book and reflect on your own leadership journey, remember that the path to mastery is not a destination but a continual process of growth, learning, and self-discovery. Embrace the challenges and opportunities that lie ahead with courage and enthusiasm, and strive to become the kind of leader who inspires and empowers others to reach their full potential. The world needs more effective and successful leaders, and I do not doubt that you have the potential to be one of them.

APPENDIX

In this appendix, we have compiled a list of recommended books and resources, leadership self-assessment tools and exercises, and case studies that showcase examples of effective and successful leaders. Exploring these resources and engaging in self-assessment and reflection can deepen your understanding of the principles and practices discussed in this book and enhance your journey toward mastering the effective and successful leader mindset. Are you ready to explore additional resources and tools to support your leadership development?

Recommended Books and Resources

Books On Leadership Principles And Practices:

"The 7 Habits of Highly Effective People" by Stephen R. Covey - A timeless classic that provides insights into personal and professional effectiveness.

"Good to Great: Why Some Companies Make the Leap...and Others Don't" by Jim Collins - This book provides insights into the leadership qualities and practices that distinguish great organizations.

"The Five Dysfunctions of a Team: A Leadership Fable" by Patrick Lencioni - A compelling story that explores the dynamics

MASTERING THE EFFECTIVE AND SUCCESSFUL LEADER MINDSET

of effective teamwork and leadership.

"Emotional Intelligence: Why It Can Matter More Than IQ" by Daniel Goleman - A groundbreaking book that examines the importance of emotional intelligence in leadership and personal success.

Books On Communication And Team Building

"Crucial Conversations: Tools for Talking When Stakes Are High" by Kerry Patterson, Joseph Grenny, Ron McMillan, and Al Switzler - This book provides practical strategies for effectively navigating difficult conversations and fostering open communication in the workplace.

"The Coaching Habit: Say Less, Ask More & Change the Way You Lead Forever" by Michael Bungay Stanier - A guide to developing a coaching mindset and effectively supporting team growth and development.

"The Art of Gathering: How We Meet and Why It Matters" by Priya Parker - This book explores the power of intentional gatherings and provides strategies for creating meaningful connections and collaboration.

*Leadership Self-Assessment
Tools and Exercises*

Self-Assessment Tools

StrengthsFinder 2.0 - A popular self-assessment tool that helps you identify your unique strengths and talents and provides strategies for leveraging them in your leadership.

The Emotional Intelligence Appraisal - A self-assessment tool that measures your emotional intelligence competencies and provides personalized feedback and development strategies.

The Leadership Practices Inventory (LPI) - A widely used leadership assessment tool that measures the frequency of specific leadership behaviors and helps you identify areas for growth and development.

Leadership Exercises

Personal SWOT Analysis - A simple exercise that helps you identify your strengths, weaknesses, opportunities, and threats and provides a foundation for personal and professional growth.

Vision and Values Clarification - A reflective exercise that helps you articulate your vision and core values and align your leadership behaviors and decisions with these guiding principles.

Active Listening Practice - An exercise focusing on developing active listening skills essential for effective communication and team building.

Case Studies: Examples Of Effective And Successful Leaders

Case Study: Howard Schultz and Starbucks
Explore how Howard Schultz transformed Starbucks from a small coffee shop to a global brand by fostering a culture of innovation, empowerment, and social responsibility.

Case Study: Indra Nooyi and PepsiCo
Examine Indra Nooyi's tenure as CEO of PepsiCo and her commitment to balancing financial performance with social and environmental sustainability.

Case Study: Mary Barra and General Motors
Learn about Mary Barra's leadership of General Motors, her focus on fostering a culture of collaboration and inclusion, and her

efforts to drive innovation in the automotive industry.

Case Study: Satya Nadella and Microsoft

Analyze how Satya Nadella revitalized Microsoft by embracing a growth mindset, fostering innovation, and promoting a culture of empathy and collaboration.

Case Study: Nelson Mandela and South Africa's Transformation

Discover how Nelson Mandela's leadership qualities, including resilience, forgiveness, and a commitment to justice and reconciliation, contributed to the transformation of South Africa.

By exploring these books, resources, self-assessment tools, and case studies, you can continue to deepen your understanding of effective and successful leadership principles and practices. Engaging with these materials will help you develop a well-rounded perspective on leadership and enhance your ability to apply these concepts in your unique context.

As you continue to pursue mastery of the effective and successful leader mindset, consider this final question: How will you use the knowledge and insights gained from this book, the appendix, and your ongoing leadership development journey to make a lasting impact in your organization, your team, and the world? By reflecting on this question and committing yourself to continuous learning and growth, you will equip yourself better to navigate the challenges and opportunities that arise in your leadership journey and ultimately make a lasting positive impact.

The resources, tools, and case studies in this appendix are a starting point for your ongoing leadership development. As you continue to grow and evolve as a leader, seeking additional materials and experiences that can enrich your understanding of leadership principles, practices, and strategies is essential.

Consider attending workshops, conferences, and seminars focusing on leadership development, as these events can provide valuable networking opportunities, fresh perspectives, and insights from other leaders and experts in the field. Additionally, keep an eye out for emerging trends and research in leadership, as staying informed about the latest developments can help you stay ahead of the curve and adapt your leadership style and approach accordingly.

Becoming an effective and successful leader is a lifelong journey. Embrace the challenges, learn from your experiences, and continuously strive for improvement. Doing so will enhance your leadership abilities and inspire and empower others to reach their full potential.

As you progress in your journey, always remember the importance of leading with integrity, empathy, and a commitment to personal and professional growth. By embodying these principles, you will become a force for positive change, fostering a culture of excellence and innovation that can transform your organization, team, and the world.

Thank you for reading "Mastering the Effective and Successful Leader Mindset." I hope you found the information in this book valuable and informative.

If you have any questions or want more information about how I can help you with your journey, please don't hesitate to contact me. You can reach me through my website at www.johnsanchez.co, by phone at 972-455-4800, or by email at info@johnsanchez.co.

I am also active on social media, so please follow me on LinkedIn, Twitter, Instagram, and Facebook for the latest industry trends, job opportunities, and company news.

Disclaimer: The information provided in this book is for informational purposes only. It should not be considered legal or professional advice. John Sanchez makes no representations or warranties of any kind, express or implied, about the completeness, accuracy, reliability, suitability, or availability with respect to the information, products, services, or related graphics contained in the book for any purpose. Therefore, any reliance on such information is strictly at your own risk.

AFTERWORD

The Journey To Leadership Mastery

Congratulations! If you're reading this Afterword, you have reached the end of "Mastering the Effective and Successful Leader Mindset." I hope this book has provided valuable insights and practical tools to help you develop your leadership skills and become a more effective and successful leader.

The path to leadership mastery involves challenges, setbacks, and opportunities for growth and learning. It requires a continuous commitment to personal and professional development and a willingness to take risks, embrace change, and learn from failure.

In this Afterword, I want to take a moment to reflect on some of the key themes and lessons from the book and offer some additional insights and perspectives on the journey to leadership mastery.

Believe In Your Potential

One of the key messages of this book is that effective and successful leadership is not an innate talent or personality trait but a set of skills and competencies that can be learned and developed over time. The first step on the journey to leadership mastery is to believe in your potential to grow and evolve as a leader.

Research has shown that embracing a growth mindset and dedicating oneself to hard work and perseverance can lead to greater achievement and success. So, believe in yourself, and cultivate a sense of optimism and possibility as you embark on your journey of leadership mastery.

Embrace Failure As An Opportunity For Growth

Another important theme of this book is the idea that failure is not a sign of weakness or incompetence but an inevitable part of the learning process. Effective leaders understand that failure is an opportunity for growth and learning, and they approach their mistakes and setbacks with a sense of curiosity and humility.

Research has shown that a willingness to embrace failure and learn from it is a key characteristic of successful leaders. By embracing failure and using it as a springboard for growth and learning, you can develop greater resilience, adaptability, and creativity as a leader.

Understand The Dynamics Of Change And Transformation

In today's rapidly changing world, change is inevitable, and leaders must know how to navigate change successfully. Effective change management can help reduce resistance to change, foster innovation and creativity, and improve organizational outcomes.

In Chapter 7, we explored the dynamics of change management

and how to lead through change and transformation.

It is essential to understand the dynamics of change, including the various stages of change, the sources of resistance to change, and the strategies for overcoming resistance and facilitating change, in order to lead through change and transformation. By developing your change management skills, you can become a more effective and successful leader in today's dynamic and uncertain business environment.

Continued Learning And Growth

As I mentioned earlier, leadership is a journey, and the path to mastery is an ongoing process of learning and growth. Cultivating a lifelong learning mindset and a willingness to seek out new challenges and opportunities for growth is essential to becoming an effective and successful leader.

Research has shown that successful leaders are continuous learners who seek out new experiences, perspectives, and feedback to improve their skills and competencies. Investing in your own learning and growth can make you a more effective and successful leader and achieve greater personal and professional fulfillment.

In conclusion, I want to thank you for reading "Mastering the Effective and Successful Leader Mindset." I hope this book has provided valuable insights and practical tools to help you develop your leadership skills and become a more effective and successful leader.

Remember, leadership is a journey, and the path to mastery will be paved with challenges, setbacks, and opportunities for growth and learning. By believing in your potential, embracing failure as an opportunity for growth, understanding the dynamics of change and transformation, and cultivating a lifelong learning mindset, you can become the kind of leader who positively impacts the world and inspires others to do so the same.

As you continue your leadership journey, seeking new knowledge and skills is vital to help you stay ahead of the curve. The world is changing rapidly, and leaders who fail to adapt will fall behind quickly. Fortunately, many resources are available to help you stay up-to-date on the latest trends and best practices in leadership.

One valuable resource is professional development programs, such as workshops, seminars, and coaching sessions. These programs can help you develop new skills, gain new perspectives, and network with other leaders in your field. Many organizations offer professional development opportunities to their employees, so be sure to check with your employer to see what options are available to you.

Another great way to stay informed about the latest trends and best practices in leadership is to read widely and stay up-to-date on industry news. Experts in the field of leadership write many books, articles, and blogs, and reading these can help you gain new insights and stay current with the latest developments.

It's also essential to seek out opportunities for mentorship and networking. Having a mentor can be invaluable in helping you navigate the challenges of leadership and providing guidance and support as you work to achieve your goals. Networking with other leaders can also help you build relationships and gain valuable insights into different approaches to leadership.

Finally, staying true to your values and maintaining a strong sense of purpose as a leader is important. In today's complex and rapidly changing world, losing sight of what's truly important can be easy. By staying focused on your values and purpose, you can maintain a sense of clarity and direction that will guide you through the challenges and opportunities of leadership.

In closing, I hope this book has provided valuable insights and practical strategies for developing an effective and successful leader mindset. Remember, leadership is not a destination but a journey. By cultivating a growth mindset, embracing failure as an opportunity for learning, and staying up-to-date on the latest trends and best practices in leadership, you can continue to evolve and grow as a leader, positively impacting the world and inspiring others to do the same.

ACKNOWLEDGEMENT

Thanking Those Who Contributed to the Creation of This Guide

Creating a book is a collaborative effort that requires the support and contributions of many individuals. I express my deepest gratitude to everyone who helped make this eBook possible.

First and foremost, I would like to thank the team at Zunch for their hard work and dedication in bringing this book to life. From the initial brainstorming sessions to the final edits, every team member was essential in ensuring this guide was comprehensive, informative, and easy to understand.

I also want to thank my colleagues in the leadership and coaching communities for their valuable insights and feedback. Your expertise and experience were instrumental in shaping the content of this book, and I am grateful for your contributions.

Finally, I appreciate the readers who provided feedback and helped us refine this guide's content. Your input has been invaluable in making this book a valuable resource for individuals seeking to find and live their purpose.

I am genuinely grateful for the support and encouragement of my family and friends throughout this process. Your unwavering support and belief in my vision have been a constant source of inspiration and motivation, and I am grateful for your encouragement every step of the way.

To the readers of this book, I express my deepest gratitude for your interest in this topic. Finding and living your purpose is one of the most important journeys you can embark upon, and I am honored to have the opportunity to share my insights and expertise with you.

In closing, I want to thank everyone who contributed to this book's creation and helped bring this vision to life. I sincerely hope this guide will serve as a valuable resource for individuals seeking to find and live their purpose and inspire you to live a fulfilling life in alignment with your unique talents, passions, and values.

ABOUT THE AUTHOR

John Sanchez

Background and Experience

As the CEO of several companies, including Zunch Digital, Zunch AI, Zunch Communications, and Zunch Staffing, I've dedicated my career to helping businesses and individuals achieve their goals. With over 25 years of experience in leadership,  coaching, and human resources, I've worked with clients from various industries, including healthcare, education, technology, and more.

As a mentor and coach, I'm passionate about helping others find and live their purpose. Everyone has a unique contribution to make to the world, and my goal is to help individuals and businesses align their actions with their purpose to create meaningful change.

Related Works and Projects

In addition to my work with Zunch-related companies, I've authored several books on leadership, coaching, and human resources. Some of my most popular works include "The Power of Purpose: A Guide to Discovering Your True Calling," "The Leadership Playbook: Strategies for Leading in Today's Complex World," and "HR 101: A Guide to Human Resources for Small

Business Owners."

I've also had the opportunity to speak at conferences and events worldwide, sharing my insights on leadership, coaching, and purpose-driven living. I'm passionate about sharing my knowledge and expertise with others, and I'm always looking for new opportunities to connect with people and help them achieve their goals.

Contact Information

If you want to learn more about my work or connect with me directly, please visit my website at johnsanchez.co. You can also connect with me on LinkedIn or Twitter for updates on my latest projects and insights.

Thank you for reading " Mastering the Effective and Successful Leader Mindset." I hope that this guide has been helpful in your journey toward finding and living your purpose, and I wish you all the best in your future endeavors.

John Sanchez
April 2023

BOOKS BY THIS AUTHOR

Unleash Your Purpose: A Step-By-Step Guide To Living A Fulfilling Life

"Unleash Your Purpose: A Step-by-Step Guide to Living a Fulfilling Life" is a comprehensive guide to discovering and living your life's purpose. In this eBook, you will learn practical strategies and tools to help you identify your unique talents, passions, and values and align them with your actions to create a meaningful and fulfilling life.

Embrace The Timeless Wisdom Of Seneca: Transform Your Life By Conquering Fear And Finding Purpose

Discover how to conquer fear and find purpose in your life with the timeless wisdom of Seneca. This insightful eBook explores the key principles of Stoicism, offering practical tools and techniques for overcoming limiting beliefs, embracing vulnerability, and aligning your passions with your purpose. Embark on a transformative journey towards personal growth and fulfillment, guided by the ancient wisdom of one of history's greatest philosophers.

www.ingramcontent.com/pod-product-compliance
Lightning Source LLC
Chambersburg PA
CBHW072150230526
45467CB00042B/1616